VIVA VIOLA!

At anchor

Turtle retreat

2

By the brook

Lazy beat

Stamping dance

Tulip time

4

Waltz

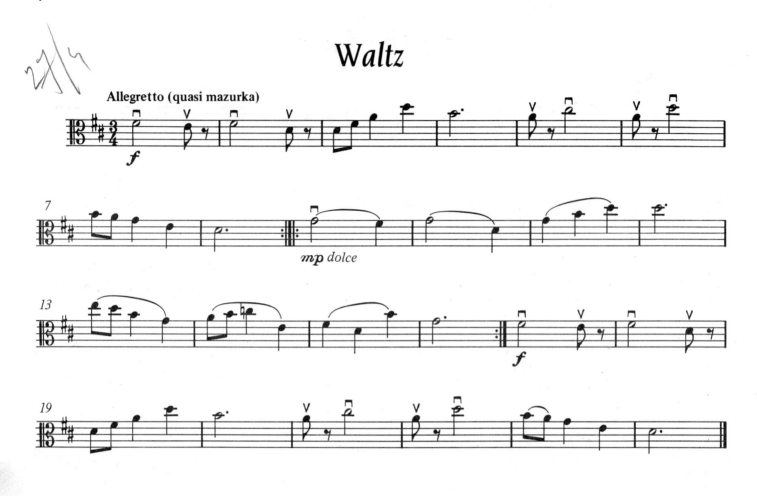

The underworld
of worms and other crawlies

Jenny's reel

On the river

6

Banana bay

Show-jumper

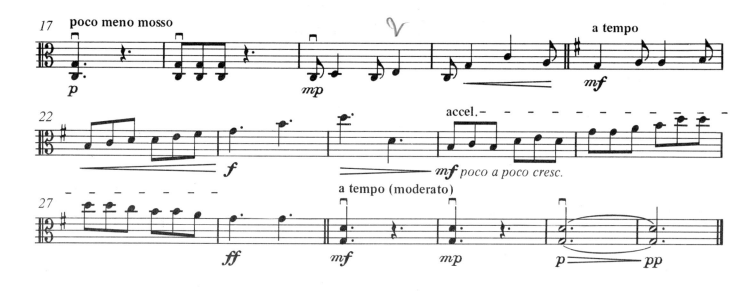

The steam train

26/3

In the mountains

Computer games

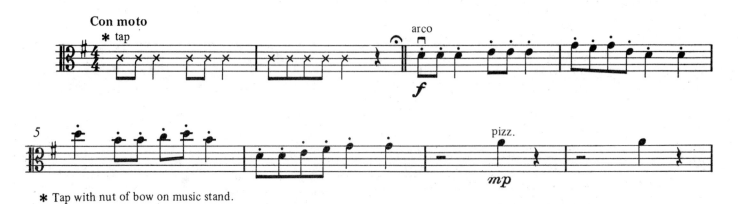

＊ Tap with nut of bow on music stand.

Poodle parade

Romans on the march

Mazurka

Ballooning

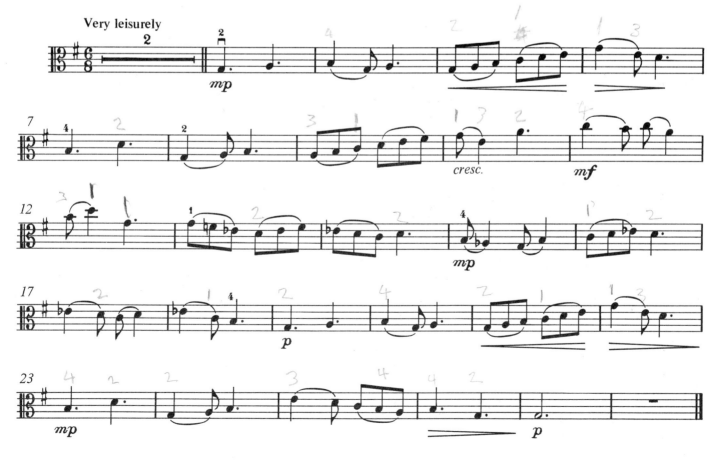

The hobby-horse

VIVA VIOLA!

20 entertaining easy pieces for viola and piano

by Marguerite Wilkinson
and Philip Bass

FABER *ff* MUSIC

All young players need simple pieces that lie well on their instrument, stimulate the imagination and are fun to play. We wanted some for viola at elementary to intermediate grade levels, but could find virtually none. So we wrote the pieces in this book, and hope that you – viola player, pianist and listener – will enjoy them.

MW/PB

Contents

© 1992 by Faber Music Ltd
First published in 1992 by Faber Music Ltd
3 Queen Square, London WC1N 3AU
Cover illustration by John Levers
Cover design by M & S Tucker
Printed in England

ISBN 0 571 51292 5

At anchor

Turtle retreat

By the brook

Lazy beat

Stamping dance

Tulip time

Waltz

The underworld
of worms and other crawlies

Jenny's reel

On the river

Banana bay

Show-jumper

The steam train

In the mountains

Computer games

* Tap with nut of bow on music stand.
** Knock on the piano.

Poodle parade

Romans on the march

Mazurka

Ballooning

The hobby-horse